THE GIRL WITH BEES IN HER HAIR

The Girl with Bees
in Her Hair

ELEANOR RAND WILNER

Copper Canyon Press

Cover art: *Field Taking Form,* by Catherine Jansen, composite color photograph, hand-colored, on Egyptian cotton, 17 × 24 inches.

Copper Canyon Press is in residence under the auspices of the Centrum Foundation at Fort Worden State Park in Port Townsend, Washington. Centrum sponsors artist residencies, education workshops for Washington State students and teachers, Blues, Jazz, and Fiddle Tunes festivals, classical music performances, and the Port Townsend Writers' Conference.

LIBRARY OF CONGRESS CATALOGING-IN-PUBLICATION DATA

Wilner, Eleanor.
The girl with bees in her hair / Eleanor Rand Wilner—1st ed.
    p. cm.
ISBN 1-55659-203-5 (alk. paper)
I. Title.
PS3573.I45673G57 2004
811'.54—DC22

                                                                2003018607

98765432

FIRST PRINTING

COPPER CANYON PRESS
Post Office Box 271
Port Townsend, Washington 98368
www.coppercanyonpress.org

To my family, originals all

ACKNOWLEDGMENTS

The Bellingham Review, Chicago Review, The Drunken Boat (online), *88: A Journal of Contemporary American Poetry, Hotel Amerika, Kalliope, Luna, Many Mountains Moving, Poetry* (Chicago), *Prairie Schooner, Quarterly West, River City, Runes, Spillway, Tri-Quarterly*

"Everything Is Starting," handset limited edition booklet by Michael Russem, Kat Ran Press, Florence, Mass., 2002

Hammer and Blaze: A Gathering of Contemporary American Poets, eds. Ellen Bryant Voigt and Heather McHugh, The University of Georgia Press, 2002

100 *Poets Against the War,* ed. Todd Swift, nthposition.com, 2003

Poets Against the War, ed. Sam Hamill, with Sally Anderson and others, Thunder's Mouth Press/Nation Books, 2003

Precessional, a limited edition artist's book by Enid Mark, The ELM Press, Wallingford, Pa., 1998

Pushcart Prize XXVIII: Best of the Small Presses, ed. Bill Henderson with the Pushcart Prize Editors, 2004

Ravishing DisUnities: Real Ghazals in English, ed. Agha Shahid Ali, Wesleyan University Press, 2000

With special gratitude: to Mary Kinzie for separating the wheat from the chaff; to superb collaborators: Enid Mark for her book artistry, Luna Pearl Woolf for her musical invention, Constance Merritt for her poetry—its call and response, Eleonora Chiavetta for bringing together *le ladre di linguaggi,* and to Catherine Jansen for her vision and her perseverance.

Contents

3   Everything Is Starting

7   Cuneiform: Meditation on a Line
9   Αντίο, Cassandra
11   Figure/Ground
13   A Short Poem about the Cosmos
14   Distances
16   Nebraska Hymn to Demeter
18   Attic Light
20   Sidereal Desire
22   Winter Conception
24   Moon Gathering
25   What Narcissus Gave the Lake
27   Orpheus on Sappho's Shore

33   The Apple Was a Northern Invention
34   Field of Vision
35   Species-pity
37   Transactions in a Field That's Overgrown
38   Multiple Image, Retro-Girlhood '40s Style
40   Musical Chairs
41   Ghazal on What's to Lose, or Not
42   Last Self-Portrait, as Rembrandt, For Instance
44   Unto the Nth Generation
46   A Moralized Nature Is like a Garden without Flowers
47   The Fossil Poet: A Post-Pastoral
49   Interview
50   Theory and Practice in Poetry
52   *"Don't look so scared. You're alive!"*
54   Pandora Jones

59 American Atlas
61 Road Taken at Evening
63 Sir Walter Ralegh, Some Time After
65 New Mexico Moon
67 So *Faux*
69 Just-So Story
71 This Straw and Manure World
72 The White-Throated Sparrow Can't Compare
73 Found in the Free Library
75 The Girl with Bees in Her Hair
77 Mnemosyne (Memory)
78 The Minimalist
80 Fetish
82 Be Careful What You Remember

87 *a space of truth blank like the sea*

89 *Notes*
93 *About the Author*

THE GIRL WITH BEES IN HER HAIR

Everything Is Starting

The snow is filthy now; it has been
drinking oil and soot and car exhaust
for days, and dogs have marked it
with their special brand of brilliant
yellow piss;
            for a week after it fell,
the snow stood in frozen horror
at the icy chill, and hardened
on the top, and then, today, the thaw:
now everything is starting
up again —
            the traffic flows, the place
where dogs pause, and sniff, becomes,
once more, invisible to us, and in
the gutters of our streets, a minor Nile
floods from the old drifts into the gasping
drains; even the sewers are jubilant
in the rush that foretells spring; the rats
dance along the pipes;
                        on all the trees,
the buds push against the sealed bark,
as if against the tight containment
of the past,
            while deep in the Florida Keys,
along some slow canal, the manatees roll
heavily in the dark stream, the way that sleepers
slowly turn in dream, and the cranes look
up, unrolling their long necks, possessed
by restlessness just before
they fly...
            light-years away, beyond the veils
of the Milky Way, out at the red edge
of creation, where everything is

always starting: there—a memory
shifts and gathers itself once more:
a memory of the time (if time it can
be called) when all that is the matter,
or all that matter is, is drawn into
one place, as if into a single thought,
and (unimaginable) ignites,
shattering the ageless night in which
the cosmos only dreamed,
and in the oldest memory
                              (of which I think
we have a share)
it was an endlessly unfolding flower
of fire—the rose of light that Dante
saw, its afterimage in the soul.
And from that flower, the seeds
of all the galaxies were
sown...
               now, in our own, the snow recedes,
the buds will shatter the end
of every twig—as everything is
starting up again—the crocus pokes
its purple, furled, above the thawing
ground,
               and when the local ember
of that first fiery bloom, our sun, touches
its silk with light, it will unfurl,
in perfect silence—unlike us, jubilant
and noisy, who never were the point,
but still delight in being
the sole narrators, upstarts of the dawn.

Cuneiform: Meditation on a Line

 = man

It begins with a story, familiar, deciphered
    from a dried language on the clay tablets
dug from the ruins of Nineveh: Gilgamesh, a bored king,
    entering the virgins of his realm as if
they were private rooms in his palace, his
    the key that opened every door; each entry
a brief spasm and a cold waking;
    like a shade walking the walls at night,
he is unable to live in the city of his own
    making, forced, by a boredom bordering
on madness, to take greater and greater
    risks, to leave more and more flesh
broken under his wheels: until Enkidu appears—
    the natural man who had been tricked (so they say)
by Ishtar's whore into losing the thick hair
    of his animal innocence; they met, ennui's king
and Enkidu; they fell, laughing, into
    each other's arms, as if the city walls
were not between them; as if Enkidu, the first
    of many "noble savages," were not
in the story to die; the inseparable
    pair enter the sacred forest of cedars, and there
(it is written) Enkidu assures his doom;
    the axe is swung, brings down the great cedar,
axis that connected the realms:
                        the slow decay
of the sound of its falling goes on
    for years, the long suspense
of the drifting feathers, bits of nest, broken eggs
    caught in the slipstream of its falling;
the scatter of light in the chaos
    of toppling leaves; the bone-deep creak

as the great trunk splits, almost leisurely,
    away from itself; then, silence—
except for the scrunch of the blunt stylus on a blank
    tablet, making the signs, wedge-shaped
like the bones of the wrist, as the hand moves
    across the wet clay, incising over and over
the fallen trunk and the three strokes that mean *man,*
    and the long wavering line that means
what must follow, and from which we descend.

Αντίο, Cassandra

> Like you, we know how the story ends,
> And still, like you, we turn the page,
> Tracing the plot to its bitter end
> In loss and the poverty of dust.
> CONSTANCE MERRITT

Like you, we know how the story ends,
but unlike you, we live past the place
of the cul-de-sac, where the old road bends
and leads on. It is paved now; you can drive
to the high seat of Delphi, climb the broken
steps: no oracle here but time, its wildflowers
fill the treasuries of vanished states, the triumph
of lizards and thistles, all that sunlight befriends
in the clear air of Greece, the gods dissolved
into lightning and stone, the drone of the locusts,
the sweet, clotted spill of the honeycomb.

And still, like you, we turn the page,
wanting the elsewhere that lives in the mind,
awed by the Lion Gate, nobility's rage,
the ironies turning like knives in the heart,
when the Furies lit the bone-fires of blood,
decisions were dire, and the sweet tramp
of hexameters made follies seem sage,
music loaned meaning: how persuasive
the intricate plot, the turn of a phrase. Still,
it was war, wasn't it, the old glory, etc.?

Tracing the plot to its bitter end
we mock our illusions, who have outlived all
but their source. For the mind tries to mend—
with the least thread from the torn garments
of grief—the story; the mourners tearing their hair
will demand a procession: we see again

the long line of people who slowly wend
their way up the stony hill of Mycenae,
tracing the storied ruins, tourists all—and
how shall we tell foresight from memory now?

In loss and the poverty of dust
we find such pleasure, obscene luxuriance
of loss, like animals who roll in dust,
we revel in remains, too long line up
to read the honor rolls of the dead, incised
in bronze, legions who died for what
seems now to us that tale told by an idiot.
We drop Cassandra's mantle in the dust.
The king will not return. The king is dead.
And look: the olives ripen, the lizards stretch.

Figure/Ground

Because it was a mystery, because there was
no church, because it happened in the first place,
she was anyone's guess, deep delving, seed-eating
Persephone; anyone's daughter—the lost one, the loved
too much, the taken away by strangers, the one
who was sweet until she ripened, the dying and
reviving one, grain sowed in the barren earth;
the one whom darkness altered, then
returned; one of the disappeared—nothing
but the dying fall of sound that might have been
a call for help or the wind turning a rusting
weathervane, the squeal
of tires on a gravel road, pebbles
hitting metal like a fall of acorns or the spray
of an automatic gun, Death punched in the mouth,
spitting its small, metallic teeth.
Equivocal seeds, pomegranate, hand grenade,
anyone's guess, this old worship of the underscape.

The Caesars, for whom the world hung like a bauble on a chain
from their thick imperial necks—when the skin began
to loosen on their frames, when fame no longer held at bay
the pain that woke them in the sweating night, when
the shadow from the sundial fell across their paths, then
from Rome they journeyed to her shrine
at Eleusis, drawn to her whom Death
dragged under but who rose up
green and tender every spring—slender hope
when tomorrow changed masters.

And she, the queen of shadows, was whatever was brought
to her: torchlight, flickering faith, resin-soaked
bundles throwing their pitch on the long walls

that turned and led on, and turned again...
far off, the barking of dogs—and close by,
only the sound of a hem brushing
rock for instruction, just the slither of skirts
and the sound of hushed breathing
in this realm of gray pastures, crimes half-forgotten
like caught wool on its bushes...

                               because it was so blurred,
because it was a mystery, because it had no book
but only a single hymn and a ruined entrance,
she was anyone's guess—death's consort, innocence
lost, last resort, amnesty's spring, stolen bride,
guide to the mass grave, its witness:
the figure who opens the ground.

A Short Poem about the Cosmos

Dark out there. Cold. Dust glimmers,
and stirs. Galaxies are born, form, spiral
in a milky swirl of light: she stands at her window
    staring out, a breeze lifts the gauze
curtain. An owl calls. She shivers a little, thinks
of gray-eyed Athena, the useless wisdom
in the aftermath of war, all the lost armies
    ghosts in iron masks — the Milky Way
like armor atomized, gone to a shimmer
of silvery dust: down to pure sheen,
glory a scatter of glitter in the dustbin of time;
    out there — old fixities, old ardors
retreating as the universe expands, just burning knots
in an openwork of stars, the galaxies
like torn lace curtains blowing
    in an empty room. In the northwest quadrant
of the sky, she sees the comet, a dirty ball of ice
thrown by some cosmic sprite, its brilliant tail
a colloquy of dust lit by the hidden sun, life-giving
    sun, the star chance threw our way.

She is shaken from her reverie
by chatter from the room next door;
the children must be playing games —
she almost shudders as she hears
it's my turn now, followed by
the clatter of the dice.

Distances

for Dorothy Roberts

The lit interior of the dollhouse rooms—
open windows that took us in:
like outcasts crouching in the snow outside,
we were enchanted by the tiny, whirling
figures in their silken luck, precious,
their pearls small as sand grains, bits of lace
at their carved throats seemed almost
to beat with life, that small pulse like
a hidden bird in the hollow just below
the neck where it opens into the spreading
wings of bone that hold the lungs,
themselves a pair of beating things,
the bellows of the great hall of the heart
that fans red embers into flame—
                              out there
the hearth, the little windows, lit, which sit
so far from us, in that dark northern Canada
of night, where silhouettes of women move
across the brilliant yellow squares of light,
and stop and bend to lift a child, or stop
to stare across the fields, across the darkened
hills, the restless stirring of the seas, across
to where we are,
                 looking back
across at them, the past
nestled in the present like a foal
in the womb of a little trotting mare that has been
dead for fifty years:
                       the stars turn, the empty
chair with its wooden spindles rocks,
a mist rises from the fields as if old Earth

itself had sighed, deeply,

                    and turned away

from the waves

that never stop eating at its sides.

Nebraska Hymn to Demeter

What we all worried most about,
living by the prairie then,
were the little ones. The grasses so thick
and standing so high, and the land
rolling like it does, if you turned
away—so many things
begging for your time—a child
might wander off, and the grass swallow her
sooner than water, without a telltale splash.
For if a child left the little path
our passing there had worn, drawn on
by this or that—a butterfly, maybe, or
a bright flower that caught her eye—
pretty soon she'd be so deep in, where
every way you turn looks just the same
and every way you go is just another place
to be lost in.
                    Back home, her mother would have
missed her, and called, and called again, and soon
the panic would spread among us 'til
we'd all be shouting, beating our way
through the tall grass; we'd fan out in the trackless
maze of thick and tangled green, and weeks
would pass before truth finally slammed
the door behind, and hope went out
for good. Sometimes, a little rack of bones
would turn up, miles or years
away, and sometimes nothing ever.

There was one mother, though, who never
would give up. Among the stalks of
wild rice and wheat, bird-carried grains
and grasses, numerous as stars, she

searched like a wind among the tall stalks,
and by the way the grasses stirred within, we knew
that she moved deep inside the prairie's heart,
and would not be consoled.
                         Though lately I suspect
she was a figment veiled in our grief, husk
of the crazy faith it spawned, like that goddess
for whom earth yawned, first took and then
gave back the dead, in a poem we read
one time in school—an oceanful of stars ago,
the prairie grass long since cut down,
and what runs underground is water now,
the sweet elixir of our tears.

Attic Light

The light moved with a kind of languor
   across the wooden floor, a slow slide
      of honey-colored fire, warming what it passed as
         it brought the grain to life: a swirl
      of spiral lines that made even the milled board
   of an attic floor into a live and speaking
thing. As the light slid across the wooden sea
   of that uneven floor, it marked
      the passage of the hours, the distant sun become
         an intimate, entering through a high
      and dusty pane, motes swarming in a slanted
   beam of veiled light, and here and there,
where wind moved a branch outside, light shivered
   as it fell and bits of it swam wildly in the wood,
      bright schools of fish in a world turned liquid by the light.

   As the hours passed, the angle shifted, long
fingers of sun slid into the corners where—like memories
   put away so long it seemed nothing could
      touch them—some dark shape was picked out by
         the light as it slid by, as if in afterthought:
      a painting, or its replica, time-darkened, in a gilded frame,
   its molding sculpted in the old elaborate
mode: it was Titian's *Danaë*, stretched out naked
   on her couch, in a trance of passion, as the shower
      of gold poured out of cloud and bathed her open
         thighs—it seemed that you could almost hear
      her sigh, and shift in her sweet unease, just as
   the last of the light that day picked out
and brightened, for a second, the rapture of her gaze,
   she who had been safely locked away, now lost
      to everything but the blinding golden fall of her desire
         and his, when time was young and matter

still inhabited by gods…and then the light moved on,
     the painting slid back into its darkened corner
in the attic overhang, and disappeared.
                                   The trapdoor
open in the center of the darkening room, the ladder
     leading, rung by rung, down into the lighted well
          of the second story, from which familiar voices
     called, seemed faint and faraway, while the late light,
as the horizon rose to blot it out, gave off the gold, life-giving
glow of that distant burning star—in the night of space,
     an island spouting fire, furious red fountain
raised against the black, insensate sky.

Sidereal Desire

Star struck   following this latter-day   Aphrodite
as she clatters   down the street   high heels
with gold glitter   on her tired feet   sparks thrown
from the friction   of dream   against the rough stone
of the real   daylight   having its way
of showing the dark roots   of even the brightest
blonde   these days   the lights stay on
there's the cool glare   of publicity   veils torn off
the body of desire   just spotty
flesh   pubic hair   shaved legs
stretch marks   a fine film of glistening
sweat   look how the stars have fallen

tonight   when she leans over the bridge
            eyes brimming with water   tired
from the constant exposure   from trying to arouse
even the memory of desire   (in times like these)
        when she stares down   eyes filling
into the dark water   on which a galaxy or more
        of stars have fallen   why there it is again

the veil! a glowing scrim of shifting moiré silks,
        silver asterisks set in motion by a wind   a blur
of stars   like a stir of bright wings in a dark air
        and the water   that was once a mirror
            is now a swirl of veils again
the stars   the gods   are taken back into the stream
        what wore our faces in an old design
drawn down   return once more to the elements
        that called them forth —
                            the veils play across the surface
of the stream   are whirled along   until they pause

some other place   a million years downstream from here
and there   the fleeting forms take shape again
        though not like ours   or anything we knew

Winter Conception

Silence in the forest's heart, and snow.
Palimpsest of trees, centuries of winter text—

bare twigs that interlock in blurred white
air, as one thought leads to the next,

half-obscured in snowy veils,
no end, though, to their reach or

to the snow; flakes thicken, the silence
deepens as they fall, lint from the pockets

of the cold, whirled to a dizziness
of white; the blizzard swallows back

the view, and every syllable of sound;
even the creaking of wood in wind

is silenced by the snow.
The wind breathes in and out

in clouds of white, the snow pure
kindness after so much noise,

so long a war of elements, of jarring
things whose natures clash, spring

back or shatter—the clang of armored
flesh, desire's fangs, the shouts

of dying men, bombed cities full
of burning souls, as Semele

who asked to see her god unveiled
saw only fire, and was consumed—

the unborn Dionysus brought to term
in the thigh of Olympian Zeus.

In whose loins will the drunken
force of life grow now, concealed

inside the falling snow, this wood
of birch and ash, as, veiled again,

the god, aroused, moves toward
another bed, and time folds back

its long white sheets of snow.

Moon Gathering

And they will gather by the well,
its dark water a mirror to catch whatever
stars slide by in the slow precession of
the skies, the tilting dome of time,
over all, a light mist like a scrim,
and here and there some clouds
that will open at the last and let
the moon shine through; it will be
at the wheel's turning, when
three zeros stand like paw-prints
in the snow; it will be a crescent
moon, and it will shine up from
the dark water like a silver hook
without a fish—until, as we lean closer,
swimming up from the well, something
dark but glowing, animate, like live coals—
it is our own eyes staring up at us,
as the moon sets its hook;
and they, whose dim shapes are no more
than what we will become, take up
their long-handled dippers
of brass, and one by one, they catch
the moon in the cup-shaped bowls,
and they raise its floating light
to their lips, and with it, they drink back
our eyes, burning with desire to see
into the gullet of night: each one
dips and drinks, and dips, and drinks,
until there is only dark water,
until there is only the dark.

What Narcissus Gave the Lake

Write what you know. And go on knowing only what
we know? And never know the lakeness of the lake?
CONSTANCE MERRITT

The lake loves what it sees, and what it sees
   is not what he saw, the beautiful boy in
the myth—for him, the water was pure reflection,
   his eyes greedily gathering back the face
that featured this image of himself, so famous
   a fixation, a tar baby to the soul, saying nothing,
holding him fast on the lake's margin.
   The lake loves him differently, darkly,
looking up and out of its own depths,
   seeing him as a path of filtered light, a sounding
line through thick green weeds that lift and sway
   their slender length, through the clouds of rising
silt, dark currents from the breeze above and
   from the springs that feed it underground;
the lake watches as the bright egg of his face wavers
   and breaks, shattering into bits and liquid
shards of light; at other times his face is jeweled
   by the brilliant fish who swim in rippling silver
schools—or mud erupts, frogs leap and break
   the surface tension on which his image rests,
and all at once, the man himself appears: a flash
   of solid flesh against a radiant, distant blue;
the water closes back. The lake sees through Narcissus
   the abundant life of its own being—for
had it not, that morning, raised its gaze
   to what, along its verge, was bent on self-regard,
it wouldn't know, as it knows now,
   what multitudes it can contain,
would not have seen how its own dark currents
   flow, nor known so many bright and darting

lives. The shifting likeness of all this was given
    to the lake, in the contemplation of
that beautiful and beauty-blinded face.

Orpheus on Sappho's Shore

A libretto for an oratorio by Luna Pearl Woolf

SONG OF THE FLOATING HEAD OF ORPHEUS:

A memory in a dream of a dismembered man,
the blue stream takes me where it will, the heavens spin
within my head: my eyes have long since
swallowed back the sky, stars, morning sun,
silhouettes that pass along the shore, the glitter of light
on the gleaming waves, a tacking ship with luffing
sails, a school of turquoise parrot fish, a run of music in my brain,
a song that burns along the nerves like fire on a string,
a dangling mirror the wind turns slowly in an empty room,
a kite-entangled cloud, a fading wish, erosion, quicksand, fog.
My heart's desire: mirage. Longing fills me still, pure
longing now, lament, bereft of figure, face, or name. Faint scent
of jasmine, floating veil, a hem of disappearing
silk, a stroke of chalk wiped off a slate.

My lyre and I float on, through seasons, centuries, the endless
permutations of the sky. The space between the stars, between the strings—
absence makes my song; and in that space, regret, like a larva in the dark,
grows fat on might-have-beens, and tunes its lyre
to loss and lack, and all forever lost in looking back; I hear
the laughter of the gods. Oh, for the sake
of what I was, whose sweet songs moved the trees to dance,
the lion to lie with the lamb, and even the stony
hearts of the gods to melt: release me now
from what I am—a cosmos in a skull
of bone, a mind awake inside a jar—
oh, pity me, cold stars, and set me free.

SONG OF SAPPHO AND THE CELEBRANTS:

We are such fools as time has made, as shade is made by bodies
mad for sun; my friends and I, shaken from our beds

of love, have come to the morning shores
of the Aegean, to wash ourselves as rosy-fingered dawn
touches the waves, and they blush;
                                    as the first sun
sets the leaves of the oak aflame—a conflagration in the heart,
we rise, like the foam-born goddess from the sea,
in a trance of froth and gaiety—today, we've come to celebrate
to the sound of wind in the hollow bones of reeds,
    in the clear light in the olive trees, the discreet silence of
lizards, the flute of the goat-footed god—the wedding of
conch shell and cithara, the meeting of island and sea.
    We'll pour libations to the gods, our sun-warmed bodies
sip the air like wine, and be immoderate in everything but sighs:

Aphrodite, spare us from the pangs of unrequited love;

ORPHEUS:

I hear the laughter of the gods.

SAPPHO:

from the vain pursuit of faded joys; from the cold, unchanging
marble dream of art—

ORPHEUS:

Oh, for the sake
of what I was, whose sweet songs moved the trees to dance,
the lion to lie with the lamb, and even the stony
hearts of the gods to melt;

SAPPHO:

   don't overcome my spirit, goddess, with longing.

ORPHEUS:

release me now
from what I am: a weary cosmos in a skull,
a mind awake inside a jar—if anyone can hear
my plea—release me, release me now…

SAPPHO:

My friends, postpone your joy an hour—

ORPHEUS:

Oh, pity me and set me free.

SAPPHO:

a mourner in a hood of bone
too long immured, implores us now
to set him free—

ORPHEUS:

   Oh pity me, cold stars, let me go free.

SAPPHO:

My friends, prepare the fire.

Drink this, nepenthe, forgetfulness,
   be Orpheus no more…

ORPHEUS:

My lyre, its incandescent strings, I leave
to the living hands that set me free;

SAPPHO:

The torch is touched to the driftwood pyre...

ORPHEUS:

this skull no longer holds my soul—transparent flame, it leaps and soars
into the wide, expanding universe,
                                        a jar of light that pours its stars
forever into darkness, filling night with fireflies, the sparks
my fiery song throws off, bright foam that flies from
the sapphire waves of an open sea... I am no more
than elegy set free, the leaping
tongues of fire, the lyre's incendiary cry:
                                        eleutheria   eleutheria

[The fire dies; Sappho takes up Orpheus's lyre]

SAPPHO:

Song-loving lyre, I take up now and sing—
my muse shall be invention, and her sisters: chance,
the sweet mundane, the sacred precincts of the olive and the vine;
I, Sappho, hear the laughter of my friends—come let us dance
to cithara and silver-throated flute, *not for us the heights
of Mount Olympos* or the dismal shades below
but on this shore, *drink honey from the sun,* and live
with an intensity so luminous—though the wind erase
the pattern that our sandals leave in sand—
I think someone will remember us in the time to come.

The Apple Was a Northern Invention

When she ate the pomegranate,
it was as if every seed
with its wet red shining coat
of sweet flesh clinging to the dark core
was one of nature's eyes. Afterward,
it was nature that was blind,
and she who was wild
with vision, condemned
to see what was before her, and behind.

Field of Vision

And if the bee, half-drunk
on the nectar of the columbine,
could think of the dying queen, the buzz
of chaos in the hive, the agitation
of the workers in their cells, the veiled
figure come again to rob the combs —
then would the summer fields
grow still, the hum of propagation
cease, the flowers spread
bright petals to no avail — as if
a plug were drawn from a socket
in the sun, the light that flowed into
the growing field would fail;
for how should the bee make honey then,
afraid to look, afraid to look away?

Species-pity

We are the saddest species that we know.
We fear the eyes of others, insects, innuendo,
and disease. We fear our own face
in the mirror, the smear of dog shit
on the shoe, the drift of snow,
the loss of face, the sneering doorman,
the turbulence at 30,000 feet, the very air
we breathe. Ease is in brochures for travel,
desire follows tracks that disappear
in sand, or water, the night sky ignores
our desperation, or feeds it hugely—
even the moon appalls us, or else we are
enthralled, watching it grow fuller, full
and white, then slip away again until
it seems no more than the scar
from where the light was taken out.

Afraid of the dark, we play with fire.
We burn, and burn.

Unfinished and unfixed as to our kind,
we never learn, however overly endowed
with mind. Lunatic and puny
as a primate goes, unfurred,
smart clay, our thumb opposed, we work
ourselves around, we change our shape
by hand, and on demand—but not-
withstanding that, we're scared, we would
be light as air, and float, unfeeling,
unafraid—
             instead, we're what we are,
the freight inside our dream
of flight—that like the *Hindenburg*

explodes aloft, and it is we who fall
from the burning clouds of wreckage
overhead; and we who drive below
at high speed in our brilliant little cars —
running over what has fallen in the road.

Transactions in a Field That's Overgrown

It is dusk in the field: uncanny, those calls,
the way that voices carry just before the air goes dark,
when the light is violet, and the eye is fooled,
just before the moon swims up from the mud
of the pond, to lie on the dark water's silken
skin, a composure that even the slightest breeze
can ruffle — the moon a shiver of minnows.

The voices have faded with the dusk,
and night has come like a curtain dropped
over the brave show of the day, the bravado
of noon, the fading certainties of afternoon,
the buzz of mosquitoes by four, the sweating of
the ice-filled glass that leaves a silver
ring on the old porch floor, as the heat
of the day wearies, relenting
by degrees, it is then, across those half-lit
fields, we hear the children call:
     Red Rover, Red Rover...
...come over, come over...
grainy as old film the memory as it goes,
as the field fades like Brigadoon, those
voices bring the dark in with them; what
twilight brought, night swallows back —

and how we ache to break and run, be
caught in those arms again, and, laughing,
fall in the evening grass, feel its damp,
all unaware, distance not yet bred of time,
and hear (*shh, don't breathe, listen...*)
our mothers' voices calling from afar
across the meadow's darkening air.

Multiple Image, Retro-Girlhood '40s Style

The cover of *Life* magazine—five out of one:
here was replication in the flesh, a litter
of five baby girls, insanity, a freak show
from that staid outpost, Canada: maples, Mounties,
snow, ice, the odd moose, Eskimos.
But now, anomaly—the Dionne
Quintuplets: their names in headlines,
Annette, Emilie, Yvonne, Cécile, Marie:
their effigies outsold the Shirley Temple doll,
everywhere, their images, always dressed alike—
five little girls, black-haired and sweet,
their birthdays in the rotogravure, and in
the ads as they grew—five little girls
in shining raincoats, patent leather bright,
each a different hue: smiling sugar
in their candy-colored coats—

    while, hovering out there, above the dark
    Canadian woods, some exiled, migrant thing
    hunting down the frozen lanes of ice, stopped
    to linger over the frame house of the Dionnes:
    five lit windows, from each the same face
    staring out, wild, through five pairs of eyes.

Their parents lost them to the State—Ontario
exploited them, put them in the province window
on display, three times a day a tourist draw,
their fivefold image sold on the auction block
to the press, the advertisers; so they grew, dressed
(like my sister and me) alike: meant to be quiet,
clean, and sweet, adorable as the Dionnes, tulip
neat, interchangeable as dolls or eggs—the Dutch girl
on the cleanser can holding the Old Dutch Cleanser can with its Dutch girl

holding the cleanser can…infinite recessional of white and
shining tiles, those gleaming bathrooms like the fields
of Northern ice—white on white on white…

One night those many years ago I had the dream.
The fields of snow, nothing nearby for miles,
one tall house set stark against the white—it looked
like a child's drawing of a house, each window
a drawn square—from which erupted flames,
red, yellow, and orange. Were others there?
Bright fire engines from a child's lexicon for help?
Adults standing around in coats, shaking their heads?
I ran into the burning house of the dream…
I rescued them, the Dionne Quintuplets, I carried
them out, I saved them all—

while up there, in the real Canada, the Dionnes
faded from view, had miserable lives, two
died young, the rest withdrew, were forgotten
by the State, the promoters, the tabloids,
the barkers at the sideshow of our times—
though somewhere in an attic
in a weathered wooden house, there is a trunk
in which five bright raincoats lie,
jewel-tones, the colors of Jell-O,
or LifeSavers in their five assorted flavors,
each with a hole in its center—the game to see
how thin you could suck it before
it shattered, leaving you with a mouth
full of momentary glass—sharp,
as if it would draw real blood,
but then it's gone—a melt
of cloying sugar on the tongue.

Musical Chairs

The chairs were set up on the hillside
so that to sit in them at all was a feat
of balance. The music came from a band
of insects—locust hum and cricket chirp,
and the steady murmur of bees in
clover. They would hush whenever a cloud
passed over the sun, its shadow sent
like an omen across the high meadow, as
warmth and color went: that's when we had
to rush and sit in the unstable chairs—one
short, of course (that's how the game is
played).
          The music resumed when the sun broke
through, the field simmering with light, but
before the hidden chorus sang again,
one more chair would be taken off.
Then round and round we went, trying to
seem at ease, but watching nervously,
elbowing others aside, wanting to be where
a place stood waiting when the sun went in,
and the music stopped. I don't know why
we thought we had to play, eyeing one another,
vying for seats on the uneven field
on which the game was played.

In earnest now, the furious tune,
its growing speed—and see,
      how one by one,
time cuts back our company,
downsized when the music
stops. Who wants to be the one
left sitting on the silent hillside now?

Ghazal on What's to Lose, or Not

for Shahid, loss beyond measure

Risk it? What, after all, have you got to lose?
With a time-honored form, you ought to lose.

Never mind if you feel yourself losing your grip—
When wrestling with angels, you've fought to lose.

Passionate error: on the horizon, a haze of heat.
Fooled by the sun, you feel too hot to lose.

Is it the Belovèd's dear form, glimpsed in the crowd?
What the heart most desires, you're taught to lose.

Sun and wind, space: a mirror turns on a string.
The empty mind's best: all thought to lose.

You will mourn for, adore, those your ancestors killed.
To relinquish their victory is not to lose.

When the soul slips its mooring, it sails beyond far.
And sense comes untied, a knot to lose.

You float down the river, watch the clouds play.
So, forgetting the game, you forgot to lose.

In all transparent modesty, you drop your name.
For Eleanor is not a lot to lose.

Last Self-Portrait, as Rembrandt, For Instance

The three birds had sat on the table by the tall
    Dutch doors for all those years — the doors
to the manicured gravel sweep of gray leading
    to the blue, magnanimous curve of a calm
and virtual sea — a brush dipped first in deep marine,
    then dipped and dipped again into the glass
of turpentine, then spread across the only slightly
    mottled surface of the white, light implicit
in the way the blue gave way to wash. While
    on the wall, slim figures held their poses
easily, so tranquil in varnished oils,
    no thoughts but turning shadows crossed
their brows, the ribbons on their hats
    caught, lifting in some long-forgotten air. A dog,
wrought-iron, gleaming in a thick and lacquered
    black, sat by the huge, cold hearth, its spectral flames
a backdrop for the burghers in their velvet coats,
    cheeks rouged by wine and firelight, while
watching, all the time, from the table by the tall
    Dutch doors, three delft birds, blue and white,
placed to catch the last long rays of sun
    as it slid into the Zuider Zee, gold mirror
in the closing hour of light. A last beam caught
    the bright bead of an eye, it gleamed — a wing
tip stirred, one bird stretched its leg, another
    fluffed its feathers out, the third one tried its voice.

The surface of the lake began to stir, the wind was up,
    the figures on the wall shook off their trance,
the dog began to bark, the stars shone in the door,
    the vines had come inside the room, the ceiling
stood open to the night, the newly risen moon shone through
    one ragged hole and was repeated in a pool of rain

that had gathered on the pocked and pitted floor.
    A match flared in the derelict and darkened house.
I saw myself, a pair of staring eyes and wild, disordered
    hair in the cracked mirror of the hall, and stood
a moment there, undone, until the match flame reached
    my hand, and light, however small, became
pure pain. I blew it out.

Unto the Nth Generation

All day something has led me on—
at times, scarcely more
than a wavering in air, a heat mirage,
as if the longed-for face
of water were reflected back
on desert air. I call it Hagar's angel,
for it is mine, I swear, when it hovers
just ahead, and it is that, not hope, that drives us
through these burning sands, the sun heavy and hot
as chains of gold, memory a sheepfold broken in
by thieves, even the past a ransacked place,
nothing of my own but a surly son
who curses fate: bitter, with his father's face,
but without his father's name—cast off, the cub
of a concubine. Yet something cares for us,
all day in a cloud of heated breath, a spirit
or a dervish made of dust; I call it Hagar's angel,
for it loves vacancy and wells and space,
our only compass now when all location's lost,
the wind dies, and the camels stumble.

The sun sinks behind the swollen hills of sand.
The temperature falls. Night harbors drifting
souls, the stars their signal fires among
the ghostly dunes. *Look, Ishmael,* I say,
there: through the open flap: how bright
that star, and next to it, the crescent
moon: how like a scimitar of light!

But Ishmael, withdrawn, does not
reply. He leaves our tent, goes out into
the desert night. The shining cloud that led us
this long day, as I watch amazed,

drops about his shoulders
like a glowing cloak, or like
some thought in which he's lost.
When he comes back inside our tent,
this flame-eyed man, I know him not.

Next day, he rides, a stranger at my side, wrapped
in heavy silence, thick as a burnoose,
against the stinging sand, my anxious eyes.
Everywhere I look, a cloudless sky
of searing blue stares back, as we move on,
drawn into this oven of a world.

A Moralized Nature Is like a Garden without Flowers

In the Garden, as the Bible tells it,
there were: two trees—forbidden;
the snake of a former cult—demoted;
one man, one woman—her appetite,
their famous shame. And nowhere
in the shade of those *verboten* trees
was there the feel of cool moss under-
foot, never the veils of water, gravity-
flung, over the edge of granite
into the dark that pools below;
no restless hours, no bug-eyed frog
unfurling its tongue, no insect hum
of propagation, no busy messengers
of change; nowhere the silken bowers of
desire into which bees plunge, drunk
on nectar and remembrance
of the larval honey-lust—
no flowers in Eden, not even one.
So beauty had no figure, no sacred
symmetry, centripetal, slowly opening
to a half-glimpsed nuclear core—
hot enough to melt the arctic,
icebound heart of God.

One flower in Eden
and they would have known
beauty, and knowing that,
would know how beauty fades.
But Eden was flowerless, and from
that lack come flaming swords,
and words like *everlasting, absolute,*
and parting seas, and burning towns,
and fear of looking back.

The Fossil Poet: A Post-Pastoral

for Dave Lee

It was long after his time on Earth
when they found him, the New Ones,
on a dig in the Place Where
the Sun Sets. They guessed that ash
from some catastrophe had caught him at his work,
for a machine, archaic, was found beside him,
open, a set of small extruded squares in rows
bearing ancient letters, and what might have been
a primitive code of numeration. Seeing him—
here in the Museum of the New Ones, themselves
extinct these many years—I found myself
strangely moved, rare in these decades of drought,
as if the dust of the world has muted our senses,
even our antennae delay their signals,
letting the moments pass, seconds empty
as the ruins of the human world.

It must have been the way time opened
its deep shaft into distance as I gazed at him,
so many eons ago this creature turned
his life to words, even as I word mine.
For as I looked, it seemed I heard
that sweet hum begin again: the sound
of early summer, when we had just
burst humming from our shells, leaving our
perfect images clinging to the walls, and stretched
our still-damp wings to dry in the dying sun.
Our larval period underground, longer
than our full-grown lives in what is left
of light, allows us to survive, and makes
our faded days seem almost bright.

But as I stared into the case in which the fossil-poet
lay, I felt some memory stir, and half revive —
a brighter sun, high pastures, gorges, rivers,
towers of rock, landscapes unlike ours
where everything is worn down flat, the dust
keeping the air a fine scrim of yellow-gray.
As if the fossil-man himself were dreaming
me, I saw his vision of the world
that used to be — alive with contours, moving
shadows at the feet of cliffs, running streams,
pine scent, a wind to make the branches sing —

but then the dream began its slow retreat
into the dust-filled air, and though I bid it stay,
it grew more dim, and what I felt
along my body's length was the ice-cold wall
of glass to which I clung. Inside, the fossil-poet
dreamless lay, petrified, unmoving in the clay.
Bearing away the loss of what he knew — with a thrust,
I pushed off, spread my wings, and flew.

Interview

Q. *Who are your influences?*
A. The poet who dressed in white and stayed in her room,
   The one who wore a turban, rings, and famously took to her bed,
   The one who killed herself, again and again, till she got it right:
   These are the ones who showed me what I should not do.

Q. *What is your personal iconography?*
A. The skull in the sand a palace for the ants; the portholes
   Of the sunken ship turned into portals for the fish;
   The lifeline of a phrase tossed over the abyss.

Q. *What can you tell us about your personal life?*
A. Does the rain have a mother?
   Is the mole the explicator of the lawn?
   (The dancer keeps the mask for calling in the gods.)
   Is the fire by night as bright at dawn?

Q. *What are your views about form?*
A. The window frames a view, but then
   Outside the frame is an immensity of blue.
   The notion of immensity depends upon the frame.
   Whatever we name, we exceed.

Theory and Practice in Poetry

for Annie, working the desk at the Canyon Ranch

The idea that freezes me this time
   is the "ideal" of a poet finding
      her poetics. While outside, Mr. T
        in his T-shirt is prowling the greens,
      and the long lazy days are lying down
   in the meadow outside the ruined
precincts of an old sophistry, in
   another state, getting on toward noon,
      where, among a thickness of flowers
        so redolent and sweet as to dizzy
      even the bees, summer slides in,
   bringing a haze of heat like the skin
shed by a river when a mist rises
   from its indolent wet back, droplets
      of water (each carrying a world)
        that travel on the back of a sequined
      wind to that meadow woven of
   grass, flowers, and guesswork—so
intricate a tapestry of greens
   that in all that steam, and heat, and
      growing matter, the *ideal of a poet*
        finding her poetics is lost like
      a ball in tall weeds, and the dog who
   finds it carries it off in his mouth,
coating it with his sweet saliva,
   and brings it, across miles of odd
      synapses and scattered thoughts,
        and drops it at the feet of a woman
      who is staring down a well, but
   just then turns away to acknowledge
the warm breath on her knee, and
   reaches down and pats the warm

furred head of the panting, eager
      dog, who feels pleased at his
    feat of fetching, as does she, as
she rubs behind his ears
and lifting the sticky ball from
   his mouth, she thinks for a minute
    of tossing it down the well, but
      instead she throws it, as far
   as she can, into the lucid blue
desert sky, and watches
as it makes that beautiful arc
  (gravity's rainbow) back
    toward the sandy earth
      as the dog hurtles off after it,
   until, all at once, all unaware
of how he has found it—there it is: bright
and round in his mouth, then dropped
   like the world at your feet.

"Don't look so scared. You're alive!"

for Marilyn Krysl

Who speaks? Now that the Muses
have traded their togas for faded rags;
now that their spring has dried up;
their once-firm breasts old dugs sagging,
their thoughts wandering into clouds
of theory, inspiration's exhaust—who
is it then wakes the writer in the night
and speaks? Now that Clear Channel
has bought up the air and fills it with
babble and gas, and Truth lies
choking in a shuttered room; now
that the Angel with the flaming sword
has put the Garden to the torch; among
shards of bone, broken tablets, a mosaic
of haphazard art, the hyenas gather,
and the tanks roll on, and the heartland
crowds cheer on cue (*the dim boy
claps because the others clap*)—

Who sings to the dying, who wraps
in her shawl the charred lexicon left
on the steps of the ruined library
next to the toppled stone lion—
who turns away in contempt
from the limousine's passing,
Folly's regent, God's shadow
behind tinted, bulletproof glass—

Who won't turn the page
to a grave for the language,
nor splinter the syntax to mimic
explosion, nor dismember sense

to appeal to sensation; who, knowing
the cliff face, the handholds, the rope,
reckless, swings out past the edge
in a wide, daring arc—
the wind there is howling,
but her feet find the ledge.

Pandora Jones

I have been tired of late, the old trunk with the rusted lock
stays closed most days, but, now and then, I lift the lid
again; it's where I keep the few things that I care to keep—

a book of myths half-eaten by the moths, my mother's sable
brushes, dried tubes of oil paint, a fur-lined cape I wore
that winter we toured Russia, and the formal gown

of taffeta—a shocking green I wore to sing the part of Eve
in the opera called *Paradise,* by a composer long since dead
and never very good; its mise-en-scène was pastoral—

a grove of painted trees hung with fat, gilded fruit,
where large-eyed lions, fox, and deer cuddled up together—
Edenic stage from which predation had been banned.

Oh, that was sweet, with all its melodies of peace, and me
entranced, engaged to a tenor in a light buff bodysuit;
our duet lavishly praised in the Paris press (which got us

the Russian tour). The bass was a tall man, who lounged
against the tree whose fruit I was forbidden—and after him,
the tenor seemed a bore, and Eden just a cardboard set,

and whoring for applause seemed all at once a trap
in which I'd stepped, its iron claws catching the fabric
of the dream that brought me there. I threw my clothes

into the trunk, half-empty now, once filled with the tools
of my father's cast-off trade: a makeup kit, a colorful
array of silken scarves and magic tricks, a rabbit

stuffed, whose glass eyes caught the light until it seemed
the very life; a deck of cards, a set of silver rings, a box
with hidden springs permitting an escape. I have been

traveling ever since. The tall bass left me somewhere
in the Alps, or I left him—I can't recall. But the snow
had begun to melt in the mountains, the air was clear

and I could breathe at last; I felt as new as a snake
must feel who's shed her skin and left it, a dry husk
for the wind to fondle. I've learned to travel light,

and leave no footprints in the snow. But still, I keep
this trunk—its magic made my father's way, and mine,
since I was the girl he sawed in half—

and while the crowd cheered and he took his bows,
I got away. I've left his tricks behind, but kept these shreds
of the life I fled when I chanced to look inside.

American Atlas

This morning the mountains were moving again,
   the train sliding across the northern steppes
      of America, clouds clinging to the peaks
         as they disappeared behind the glass, one
            after the next. The trees, up close, went first,
         just green streamers at this speed,
      and, it is true, the mountains lasted longer
to the view—but still they went. The roof
of the train was glass, and the windows
   huge, so that the moving landscape was
      the sheath of our cocoon—everywhere we
         looked, the world streaked by. At night, safe
            in the rocking bassinets of berths, we
         could forget how the world was fleeing,
      a fugitive from our gaze—the fields turning
to malls and parking lots, then those a blur
of asphalt and of lights; the forests
   rushing past on the flatbeds of logging trucks;
      the transient cities were a smear of
         toxic gold, a yellow pall that flowed by us
            like buttery, liquid smoke. The Vs
         of geese retreated through the skies;
      we saw no animals at all, and if, out there,
   birds called or insects chirped,
we heard nothing through the walls
   of glass. Sometimes we wandered down
      the narrow swaying line of cars,
         the tubules of our sealed world; a blast or two
            of air would hit us as we swung between
         the cars—freezing air, and thin, that forced
      us quickly back inside. Days passed,
   and months, and then the years, as we
watched the world fly by, and disappear;

and lately we have noticed that the blur
        out there is getting worse, but whether
            this is a symptom of our failing eyes, or
                the earth itself is going dry, its thick loam
            turned to dust and blowing in the wind, a desert
        where the woods and farms once stood, or
    the world outside is somehow growing shy —
at times it seems to abruptly turn away — the train on a hairpin curve,
    the fleeing world the product of our speed.
        But it is when the mountains shift on their great
            pedestals of stone and, one by one, begin
                to slip away, that a desolate thought
            will rear its head — as if a giant had grown tired of
        its burden of the sky…a cry goes down the cars
    and here and there we hear the fists
beating helplessly against the panes, for knuckle-
    bones will shatter long before the glass gives way.
        Someone pulled the high red handle of the emergency brake.
        The handle came off in her hand. We hurtle on.
            The mountains are going now, faster and faster
        they seem to race away from us, like waves
    in a strong ebb tide from a fading coast —
we stare at what is happening out there;
as daylight will dispel a ghost, nothing now
    impedes our view, and someone shouts:
        A toast! Let's drink to that. Prosit! and lifts
        an empty glass to the empty air.

Road Taken at Evening

As the shape of a line or a road taken at evening
leads away, and also accidentally toward...
so the long road out of the self (the one that Roethke
marked for us in going) goes often to the edge
of a kind of emptiness: imagine endless mist or
gray cloud never giving way to solid land
or sea. A window on that void, and inside, a babble
of voices, the clink of glasses, an occasional phrase
that cuts a groove of sense..."I saw it fall..."
"tax breaks," "in whose defense..." "And did you think..."
And there is grief at the table where you sit,
a grief engendered by, or else engendering,
that void. This was the place you thought, for
so long, to avoid, and then that road, taken
at evening, brought you back to where it was.

Here, no slightest thing: no leaf, no velvet sheen
on petal or on skin, no sharp detail
of sculptured limb—
no bulging vein or incised fold, no shred
of silk or shard of china with
its partial rose—
                    here is but the vacant place
to which the evening road has led:
an evening out of what had been so various,
so opulent in its details, such an excess,
such persuasive digressions, dune grass,
scurrying mice, molasses in a jar, foaming
beer, Antigone rescued in time, Icarus landing
in a Tuscan field among the wildflowers—
such a delirium of gratified desire.

And now, lost in the flowers of memory
that grow with such profusion in the mind,
the gray expanse seems broken by a hand
that wipes a fogged-up window clear—
and those are stars out there
and we are less than nothing to
that Libra balancing her scales in the dark.
She needs no blindfold on her eyes;
our justice is not even gold dust in the scales
of space, its seething energies, its quantum
pairs the mayflies of the universe—
these scales beyond all but our numbers
to conceive. How good it is
. these days not to believe
in our importance,
for how else can we breathe?

Sir Walter Ralegh, Some Time After

She is gone, she is lost, she is found, she is ever fair.

The Bloody Tower is full of tourists now, history
gone tame—but the view of the river
is the same: same slow brown wash of tides,
the baring of the flats, their smell, their vanishing
again when the waters rise. He walks
the stony floors, puts a hand to the damp
walls, his mind devoid of rhymes
    that have come, that have gone...
as he stares out at the Thames;
El Dorado, which once burned in his mind
like the City of God, has paled to a wan
hope to save his neck from the headman's
axe. It is all wiles now, meanwhiles,
and walls. How he schemed to be free,
whose will was all for risk, and girls,
and blazing gold—but as the rivers
run in the grip of gravity, so too the force—
that neither charm, nor gifts, nor
favors of a queen can but postpone
an hour—*Tell beauty how she blasteth;*
    tell favour how it falters...
will carry all away, the waters
rush with fresh abandon
through the breach when the dream breaks,
the queen turns her back, the king
condemns, the walls drip, and at hope's
end, the Orinoco flows, at whose
headwaters El Dorado once thrust
its blinding towers through the clouds—
    But true love is a durable fire... Never
    sick, never old, never dead...
On that last voyage out—he sick at the river's

mouth, his son dead in a futile fight,
his party gone on ahead: the company of ragged
men row on upstream, drawn
by the last faint glimmer of gold...
  Go, soul, the body's guest,
  Upon a thankless arrant...
the roar of distant, pounding thunder grows,
as if a god had made the Earth his drum;
the din explodes inside their heads
as they approach, the boat tossed in the boiling
river's grip... *So did my heart dissolve*
  in wasting drops...
    Then floods of sorrow
    and whole seas of woe / The banks
    of all my hope did overbear...
  The voyage upstream ends at a wall
of water, water falling through the air
from a cliff so high the eye cannot
fathom it;
        the waterfall seems to issue
from the sky, and drops straight down
into the cauldron its fall from that great
height churned up, a maelstrom of foam—
diamonds sparkle in the fuming
spray, and chips of golden
sun play in their wake as they turn back,
and float downstream...
              Ralegh thinks of Orpheus,
his severed head, its pallbearers the waves, while
yet it lives, and sings: *Go, since I needs must die,*
  And give the world the lie.

Beyond the roar of the waterfall, upstream,
in the abiding dusk and rustle
of the rainforest floor, the old gods
tip their arrows with gold,
a monkey screams.

New Mexico Moon

Y la luna.
Pero no la luna.
Los insectos.
Los insectos solos,
crepitantes, mordientes, estremecidos, agrupados,
y la luna…
          FEDERICO GARCÍA LORCA

Too heavy to move in the wind, the piñata
hung there while the leaves played around it,
a small ram, flaunting its cardboard horns
and a coat of crepe paper, curled and glued,
as many-hued as Joseph's coat, bright
signal of one chosen by the father
for sacrifice.
          The moon, meanwhile, made
its lunatic transit of the sky, as full of empty
suggestion as a surrealist game, and as compelling
to the eye, that cavern of hunger for sense.
The ram went on hanging there, waiting
for the candles to be lit, the party to begin.
The wind whispered to it in Spanish
     una brisa triste
and, nearby, the pale branches
of the paloverde nodded in agreement.
Underground, the tarantula stirred in its hole,
but that, no one heard, *nadie.*

The little ram is stuffed with sweets
meant to rain down
mock manna from heaven —
though to get it, the player
must wear the blindfold,
and, with the thick wooden stick,
and everyone shouting, swing and swing
at the air.

When, at last, the stick
has had its way with the papier-mâché,
and the shower of candy is finished,
and the hollow, torn body of the ram
is left on the ground, ignored
even by ants,
                    the moon
that hung in the branches
like a halo behind the small animal's
head, slips now behind mountains
     Huye luna, luna, luna
and on ten thousand cheap pots,
T-shirts and postcards, the coyote
raises his face to the heavens, and howls.

So *Faux*

And so it piles on
and piles up, and comes across
time's tundra in the dull thunder
of its coming on, with a glacier's
glum imperative to move,
and as it does, it adds (though
slowly) up
                    until the sum
of all that now accumulates
can strike one dumb, a bronze
gong in a field of stone,
that echoes and reverberates
till sense itself is numb,
a thorn driven into a statue's
thumb; what comes of endless
iteration, like a reappearing
image in a hall of mirrors
that shrinks as it accumulates,
receding like the smile
on the anchorman, a slice of white
the screen fades slowly into
gray, as a waning moon
retreats into the clouds —
cumulonimbus piling overhead,
a ghostly herd of buffalo,
or the tumulus of some expired
god, dead and buried in
a spectral beehive tomb
aloft in the evening sky, until
the clouds let go a crystal shower,
the cold sky fills with snow
that falls inside the shaken globe
held in a moving hand; under

the dome of glass, the tiny
replica, gowned in fluted gray
and wearing her little crown, lifts
her torch among the glittering bits,
welcoming the artificial snow.

Just-So Story

Do not make treaties with these people.

TRANSLATION OF NAVAJO MESSAGE INSCRIBED ON THE DISK
LEFT ON THE MOON BY NASA

It is very quiet on the moon. A cat squarls —
but that is back on Earth, on streets of stone
where sound echoes: trashcans tipped over,
glass breaking, fear in a gray overcoat firing its
guns; it is all metal on metal — a plumber's snake
trying to shed its iron skin, clanking, sparks
flying; a steel beak hatching out of an egg
of glass, the cracking shell a shatter of ice
in the ear. While on the moon, an airless peace:
the craters aglow with distant sun, and nothing
to disturb the quiet dust.
                              In a grove deep in the past,
when the ibex was still bidden by its image drawn
with a stick in the sand — a lion came down to drink
where the moon lay, white and naked, on the pond,
trails of light around her, a corona of snakes.
The lion was very thirsty, and it drank and drank,
until the pond was dry, and the moon the barest
glimmer on the mud. And that is how darkness
first escaped from the place where it had lain
on the bottom of the pond.
                              Now, the blood
from the kill no longer returns to the gods
so nothing is lost, but spills
in the road for the jackals to drink.
In the silence of the moon, Old Glory forever
flies in its fixed imitation of a flag in wind,
a permanent wave that can't disappoint
the eager cameras of the press by hanging limp
in the airless atmosphere of conquered space.
Far below, the busy cameras snap the photo op:

a President, drawing his brows together
in the fixed imitation of a mind at work.
Down all the streets nearby, the wind rips
at the trash, you can hear the sound of
shredders in the shuttered rooms. Dogs bark.
The subway shakes the sidewalk grates.
Everywhere, the dark ascends
by stairs, by escalators, up through manholes
with their covers pushed away. Even by day,
though just a bit more slowly, the dark extends
its sway. The rats are growing bolder now;
you can hear the steady sound of gnawing
where they have dragged the last bright crust
of moon into their hole.

This Straw and Manure World

And the mare kicks at her traces, pulling the old-fashioned rig
around Independence Hall, surrounded now by cheap aluminum
stands, fences to hold off terrorists, another fool's errand on which
Smokey the Bear and his brethren, with their self-important official hats,
have been sent: the terrorists don't give a damn about our little historic
pile of bricks and sentiment, from a time before empire, when
18th-century men, in what was hopefully called the Enlightenment, made
their stand for autonomy, more economic than ideal, but sanctified
                    by time
and by an empire's need for roots with some morality clinging to them—
not just dirt. There was a prediction, back in Franklin's time, that if
the population grew at the current rate, the amount of horse manure
would be, in another century, 18 feet deep. They weren't entirely wrong.
Though they didn't factor in the steam engine, Henry Ford, or the
                    trolley car,
they guessed right on the depth of horseshit, though most of it is in D.C.,
where it draws crowds of flies; where the Washington Monument, white
                    towering obelisk,
glowers with its red electric eyes, a Klansman in a white hood,
staring down the blossoming Mall, admiring its reflection in the
                    monumental pool.

The White-Throated Sparrow Can't Compare

for Tony Hoagland, with thanks for the images

He had made it through so many winters,
an optimist in the blizzard's heart, staying on—

so it seemed wrong, unfair (if such a word
has any currency), that the gray expanse
that used to mean the rain of spring
should be the solid metal of a sky
in motion overhead, and nowhere
for a small and singing thing to fly,
now that the bombers had come back,
a phalanx overhead, a Roman legion
given wings, and the land below
grown dark—the way a shadow slips
across the land when a cloud passes
overhead. But there resemblance ends.

As does ours with the sparrow, who, resting
on a shaded branch, shakes his wings
and gives the clear, reflective whistle
for which his kind is known.

And now the very thought of him
has flown; the mind can't hold for long
the sparrow and the bombers
in a single thought. Mad
to make them share a line, as if
to balance power so unequal
on the creaking fulcrum
of the merest *and:*
                    a pennyworth
of weight with its live, pensive song
against a roaring overhead—pure dread,
its leaden tonnage, and its tongue.

Found in the Free Library

Write as if you lived in an occupied country.
EDWIN ROLFE

And we were made afraid, and being afraid
we made him bigger than he was, a little man
and ignorant, wrapped like a vase of glass
in bubble wrap all his life, who never felt
a single lurch or bump, carried over
the rough surface of other lives like
the spoiled children of the sultans of old
in sedan chairs, on the backs of slaves,
the gold curtains on the chair
pulled shut against the dust and shit
of the road on which the people walked,
over whose heads he rode, no more aware
than a wave that rattles pebbles on a beach.

And being afraid we forgot to see
who pulled his golden strings—how
their banks overflowed while
the public coffers emptied, how
they stole our pensions, poured their smoke
into our lungs, how they beat our ploughshares
into swords, sold power to the lords of oil,
closed their fists to crush the children
of Iraq, took the future from our failing grasp
into their hoards, ignored our votes,
broke our treaties with the world,
and when our hungry children cried, the doctors
drugged them so they wouldn't fuss,
and prisons swelled enormously to hold
the desperate sons and daughters of the poor.
To us, they just said war, and war, and war.

For when they saw we were afraid,
how knowingly they played on every fear—
so conned, we scarcely saw their scorn,
hardly noticed as they took our funds, our rights,
and tapped our phones, turned back our clocks,
and then, to quell dissent, they sent
(*but here the document is torn*)

The Girl with Bees in Her Hair

came in an envelope with no return address;
she was small, wore a wrinkled dress of figured
cotton, full from neck to ankles, with a button
of bone at the throat, a collar of torn lace.
She was standing before a monumental house —
on the scale you see in certain English films:
urns, curved drives, stone lions, and an entrance far
too vast for any home. She was not of that place,
for she had a foreign look, and tangled black hair,
and an ikon, heavy and strange, dangling from
an oversize chain around her neck, that looked
as if some tall adult had taken it from his,
and hung it there as a charm to keep her safe
from a world of infinite harm that soon
would take him far from her, and leave her
standing, as she stood now — barefoot, gazing
without expression into distance, away
from the grandeur of that house, its gravel
walks and sculpted gardens. She carried a basket
full of flames, but whether fire or flowers
with crimson petals shading toward a central gold,
was hard to say — though certainly, it burned,
and the light within it had nowhere else
to go, and so fed on itself, intensified its red
and burning glow, the only color in the scene.
The rest was done in grays, light and shadow
as they played along her dress, across her face,
and through her midnight hair, lively with bees.
At first they seemed just errant bits of shade,
until the humming grew too loud to be denied
as the bees flew in and out, as if choreographed
in a country dance between the fields of sun
and the black tangle of her hair.

                        Without warning
a window on one of the upper floors flew open—
wind had caught the casement, a silken length
of curtain filled like a billowing sail—the bees
began to stream out from her hair, straight
to the single opening in the high facade. Inside,
a moment later—the sound of screams.

The girl—who had through all of this seemed
unconcerned and blank—all at once looked up.
She shook her head, her mane of hair freed
of its burden of bees, and walked away,
out of the picture frame, far beyond
the confines of the envelope that brought her
image here—here, where the days grow longer
now, the air begins to warm, dread grows to
fear among us, and the bees swarm.

Mnemosyne (Memory)

Mnemosyne, according to Greek tradition, was mother
of the Muses, who inspired the arts of humankind.

Mnemosyne rises like a geyser from the hissing
spring; she calls her mourning daughters to her side—
the long-haired Muses, on whom the old bards
called when, taking lyre in hand, they gave
heroic measures to a dying world,
to war—a story and a musical score,
for brothers dead at each other's hands—
choral odes of praise:
Victory has come to Thebes!

In shame, the Muses turn away, tend
only the wounded now, their once-bright
garments filthy and torn; bits of glass,
shrapnel and bone in their hair, gray
with age, horror, the dust of mortar blown
from demolished rooms; exposed to air, the torn
mesh of deserted looms turns
to grimy cobwebs, catching bits of ash
and flesh; Memory's daughters
keen and tear their hair, while nearby,
drunken men piss into the ditch, then raise
the bucket from the local well to use
for target practice, and as the last of the water
dribbles through the holes—Amnesia,
dumb sister of Mnemosyne, brings her daughters
forward, offering them to the sons of men,

that they *long remember nothing*
neither wind nor wake.

The Minimalist

The man in the flannel shirt has come to fix
the hearth. Loose bricks in the chimney, the swift's
deserted nest, the grime smoke left
in its hurry to ascend. He stands inside
the fireplace, looking up.
                          The flue
had been closed for years, stuck shut
now, sealed from the residue
of time, and from disuse, scant passage,
like the doors of the dead in Umbria, bricked in,
unsealed only to carry out the corpse,
the shell of one who lived within. After,
it is sealed up again.
                      As when
the door of the dead is opened in the heart,
and someone else who once lived there
is carried out; then, brick by brick,
numb by never, the door is sealed shut
once more.
          The man is standing in
a hail of brick dust, a storm of ash,
debris. When he steps out of the hearth,
he is gray as the limestone statues
that line the garden paths — hair, skin,
and clothes, all gray. He shakes himself,
like a dog coming out of a lake. He asks
for a paper, and pen; sits down at the hearth's
edge, in the rubble from the open draft,
and draws a square. He fills it in with blue.

Later, he darkens the blue. He dips his finger
in the white-gray ash in which he sits,
and slowly, as if everything depended

on the simple thing he drew,
he traces a circle of white within the square—
the ghost of fire in the circle of ash
in a square of midnight blue.

Fetish

Fetish is defined by
Slavoj Žižek (a philosopher
writing from Vienna)
as the embodiment of the Lie
that enables us to sustain
an unbearable truth. We cling
to the disavowal of what is so
in the shape of an object
that we love and can't let go—
this object lets us go on
as it keeps the full impact
of what is real
from reaching us. Though
he says so, in the fetish of his
nomenclature, he too is hiding
from the nature of the sentient
beast. Mind-numbing
numbers massacred, year
after year, by our own kind,
more kin than kind – how
live with what we know
without the Fetish, pale
as hope, evanescent
as the foam, translucent wings
made in the image factory
of that recurrent dream
where madness is staved off
another day. While real
cities fall in burning chunks
of concrete, melted steel
and flesh, who dares
(philosopher or not)
to mock the glued-together

toothpick cities of the heart,
where the soul, that cricket,
lives and chirps, and leans
against the brittle wood,
and, as a Fetish should, even
in the twilight of the gods, folds
back its little wings, and rubs
its skinny legs against
the odds, and sings.

Be Careful What You Remember

Can you see them now—the statues?
Can you see them, stirring on their pedestals,
trying out their stiff arms, stepping gingerly
down, breaking the glass walls that encase them?

At the Vatican, forcing the door of the locked
room, tearing off the plaster-of-Paris fig leaves,
rummaging about in the heaps of broken-off
genitals, so that, when they leave God's palace of art,
like the eunuchs of China's final dynasty, who left
the palace for the last time, carrying in small jars
the parts of themselves taken by empire—
so, too, the statues would be whole now, heading home.

They tear themselves from the fountains, leaving
behind the public play of the waters; climb down
from their candlelit niches, deserting
their place in the great composition. They enter
the long loneliness of roads, their exodus making
a path from the cities, a gleaming white stream
like refugees returning to their distant, burned villages,
their memories a desolation of marble.

Day and night they travel—some leading the horses
on which they've been mounted for years in piazzas,
their postures heroic. All are on foot, even
the gods, unaccustomed to walking; and angels
from tombstones—their wings hanging useless,
scholars and poets, tall women in togas, a boxer
with a broken nose, a hooded woman stumbling
under her son's dead weight, an armless Venus,
a headless Victory led by Justice—the blindfold
torn from her eyes. Their streams converging

on the road to the mountains, they climb higher
and higher, like salmon returning to the waters
that spawned them: the statues,
relentless, make their way to the quarries
from which they were hewn—the opened veins
in the heart of the mountain.

An avalanche heard from a distance, rumbling
and thundering, or an earthquake, a war begun,
or a world ending—we could only guess
what we had heard. Then word spread that the statues
were missing: the fountains, the squares, the galleries
stood empty; the gardens were vacant,
the pedestals naked, the tombstones abstract.
And, it is true, where the quarries had been
(you can travel there and see for yourself)
the mountain is whole again, the great rift closed,
and young trees grow thick again on the slopes.

a space of truth blank like the sea

extends itself, spaced out across the retina,
across the arc of the planet's curving flank,
the surface sliding silent in the moon's obliquities,

reclining on its shimmering depths, the layers
darkening as they descend, blank truth as far
as it goes: a blue-green mirror, cloud-shadowed

from the sky, reflection unalloyed, a passing breeze
scarcely an annoyance to its calm; a ruffled moment,
then, at once, the surface settles back again,

as the horizontal gaze is drawn out far
across those waves that rise and fall,
rise and fall as if forever; like all unspoken

truths, they give back only what they are.
The rest — reflection, fish, and tricks the mind
plays when the vista is horizon, vision is

at rest, the instruments of time laid down;
extension, flat and sweet, unbroken by
the ominous fin, or by the banner of a distant

ship, or by a far-off point of land where
a curl of smoke rises like a call for help.
There is just silence, imperturbable…

the vast, unhuman lovely reaches of the sea.
Beware the use of words that would betray
the silence that they carry in their waves,

silence like the holes that transform thread
to lace, that make of light a figure in a filigree
endowed with all the beauty of a web

without the lethal spider at its heart.
Free of predators, unfettered creatures
that the silence seemed to spawn, ride

the ocean currents, clear the air of sentences,
of words murmured over the condemned
in an old pretense of prayer. And if, just here,

a dolphin splits the calm serene of blue,
the fissure, momentary, disappears—
a flash of leaping flesh—the calm returns

as if it never were disturbed; exuberant
within this seeming blank—unlettered,
self-possessed—life swims. A window

open on the sea, out there, blue wave on blue,
beyond—more blue; a chair scrapes, breaks
the spell. Words spill: So little time. So much to do.

Notes

"Everything Is Starting" is for Marcia Pelletiere.

"Cuneiform: Meditation on a Line" refers to, and partly retells, the tragic epic of Gilgamesh, older than Homer or the Bible, and the first (extant) recorded response of the soul to life in the city, to our deforestation of the Earth, and to the grievous truth of mortality. Broken clay tablets on which it was written were first excavated in the nineteenth century from the ruins of the palace of Nineveh; the epic is Sumerian in origin, and dates back to at least 2000 B.C.E. Gilgamesh was the legendary king of Uruk, a city between the Tigris and Euphrates Rivers in what is now Iraq. My own introduction to the epic was through Herbert Mason's moving verse adaptation published in 1970 by Houghton Mifflin. My poem was originally written for Anne Guzzardi.

"Αντίο, Cassandra" — The poem's form is a glosa in reverse. A glosa prescribes that each ten-line stanza end with one of the lines from the quatrain epigraph, and that lines three and seven rhyme with it. Since I can't write if I know how something ends, I opened each stanza with the quoted lines, and reversed the form. The poem was written in a "call-and-response" exchange of poems with Constance Merritt, as were "Transactions in a Field That's Overgrown," "Road Taken at Evening," and "The Minimalist." Αντίο is demotic Greek for "goodbye."

Eight poems, beginning with "A Short Poem about the Cosmos" and ending with "What Narcissus Gave the Lake," are from a suite of poems, written for a collaboration with book artist Enid Mark, whose lithography and hand-set book design elegantly presented them in a limited edition published by ELM Press in 1998 under the title *Precessional*. The title refers to a third circular motion of the Earth, called precession, a motion less observable than Earth's daily spin or its annual rotation around the sun, and whose effects are very long term as measured by human lifetimes, and change the very stars by which we navigate and under which we are born.

Precession is caused by the fact that the tidal forces of the sun and the moon distort the shape of Earth, giving it uneven bulges on both sides. The gravitational pull of sun and moon on this misshapen sphere cause its axis of spin—the line passing through its north and south poles—to slowly move in a large circle.

Among the effects of this motion are a gradual shift in the stars, so that 2,000 years hence the star now over the north pole, Polaris (already a bit off center), will not be the North Star; another will be in its place. By the same precessional shift, the constellations on the zodiac change their position over the same timescale. Two thousand years ago, when the Egyptians and Greeks were making up their astrological tables, which we still use today, there was a different birth constellation than there is now for each month.

Some scholars claim that there is distinct evidence in the earliest mythic stories and epics that the ancients were aware of this motion, concerned about it, and hoped that this flight of stars might be reversed and "the world set back upon its axis."

In "Distances," two images—of women silhouetted in lit windows in the Canadian night and of the little, long dead, pregnant mare—are borrowed in tribute from poems in Dorothy Roberts's *In the Flight of Stars* (Goose Lane Press, New Brunswick, Canada, 1991), written when she was in her eighties.

The epigraph to "What Narcissus Gave the Lake" closes Constance Merritt's poem "Ars Poetica," from *A Protocol for Touch* (University of North Texas Press, 2000).

"Orpheus on Sappho's Shore" was written as a libretto in collaboration with composer Luna Pearl Woolf, whose oratorio was presented on April 12, 2002, at Smith College. The meeting of the two poets, the mythical Orpheus with the historical Sappho, is, of course, our invention, though a version of the legend has it that the still-singing head of Orpheus floated out to sea and washed up on the island of Lesbos, Sappho's home island and a center for poetry in the ancient Greek world. The italic lines in Sappho's songs are her own; her work exists only in brilliant fragments; little is known of her life, her various biographies being largely fiction.

"The Fossil Poet"—This poem is for David Lee, who was my guide to the petroglyphs at Parowan Gap in Utah, which inspired this proleptic imagining in geological time.

"Don't look so scared. You're alive!"—This title is the last line of a poem by Amy McNamara, and was written in a *renshi* (poem chain) with her, Donna Henderson, Sally Molini, and Ethna McKiernan. The quoted line, "The dim boy claps because the others clap," is the first, and hence thrice-recurring line in a villanelle, "The Freaks at Spurgin Road Field," by Richard Hugo, from *What Thou Lovest Well, Remains American* (W.W. Norton, 1975).

"Pandora Jones" was written in a gift exchange with the student poets in Writing Arts 302: "The Art of Poetry" (Alisa, Andrew, Bassel, Jan, Jenn, Jim, John, Kaitlin, Mary, Nick, Patrick, Ron), Fall quarter 2002, Northwestern University.

"Sir Walter Ralegh, Some Time After"—The italic lines in this poem are scattered remains from "The Ocean to Cynthia," "As you came from the holy land," and "The Lie" by Sir Walter Ralegh.

"New Mexico Moon"—The lines in Spanish are from the poems of Federico García Lorca: the first quotation is from "Luna y panorama de los insectos," in *Poeta in Nueva York;* the second, *una brisa triste,* is from the memorable last line of "Llanto por Ignacio Sánchez Mejías"; the third is from "Romance de la luna, luna" from *Romancero gitano.*

"Just So Story"—The reference to Old Glory "in its fixed imitation of a flag in wind" is literally true. The flag the astronauts planted was constructed with a permanent wave since the lack of air on the moon meant that a real flag would just go ingloriously limp.

"This Straw and Manure World"—This title is the last line of a poem by Kathleen Jesme, and is from a *renshi* (poem chain) with her and Carlen Arnett.

"The Girl with Bees in Her Hair" is for Janet Shaw, who sent the envelope.

"Mnemosyne (Memory)" — The line *Victory has come to Thebes!* is bitterly ironic, as it comes from Sophocles' tragedy *Antigone*. The reference is to the end of a struggle over the rule of Thebes by the sons of Oedipus, Antigone's brothers Eteocles and Polynices, who killed each other in the battle for domination, bringing ruin to their uncle, Creon, whose first edict, that the challenger Polynices be left unburied, set the tragedy of Antigone in motion. Thebes is a city born in blood, as it was founded by Cadmus, he who sowed the serpent's teeth, which grew into a field of armored men, soldiers who proceeded to slaughter one another, much like the brothers in the later chapter of the city-state's violent history.

The closing quotation is from the last lines of Howard Nemerov's poem "Writing" (*The Collected Poems of Howard Nemerov*, The University of Chicago Press, 1977, pp. 202–3), though I have changed the number of the verb "remember" to fit an altered context. Nemerov's poem had earlier compared the act of writing with the scoring of the blades of skaters on a frozen lake; he ends the poem thus:

> Not only must the skaters soon go home;
> also the hard inscription of their skates
> is scored across the open water, which long
> remembers nothing, neither wind nor wake.

"a space of truth blank like the sea" — This title is quoted from *From the Beast to the Blonde: On Fairy Tales and Their Tellers* by Marina Warner (Farrar, Straus and Giroux, 1994, p. 391). It appears in her discussion about the paradox of writers' awareness that words, their instruments, are capable of great fraudulence, and, in this regard, she quotes Derek Walcott, late in his book-length poem, *Omeros* (Farrar, Straus and Giroux, 1992, p. 296), praising the impartial erasures of the sea, "a wide page without metaphors," to which Warner adds, with the charm of contradiction, this lovely simile: "a space of truth blank like the sea."

About the Author

Eleanor Rand Wilner is the author of five previous books of poetry—including *Reversing the Spell: New and Selected Poems; Otherwise;* and *Sarah's Choice*—as well as a translation of Euripides' *Medea,* and a critical book on visionary imagination, *Gathering the Winds.* Her awards include the Juniper Prize for Poetry, two Pushcart Prizes, and fellowships from the MacArthur Foundation, the National Endowment for the Arts, and the Pennsylvania Council on the Arts. She holds an interdepartmental Ph.D. from Johns Hopkins University, and teaches peripatetically: most recently at The University of Chicago, Northwestern University, Smith College, and the MFA Program for Writers at Warren Wilson College. She is a lifelong activist for civil rights and peace.

Copper Canyon Press wishes to acknowledge the support of
Lannan Foundation in funding the publication and distribution
of exceptional literary works.

LANNAN LITERARY SELECTIONS 2004

Marvin Bell, *Rampant*

Cyrus Cassells, *More Than Peace and Cypresses*

Ben Lerner, *The Lichtenberg Figures*

Joseph Stroud, *Country of Light*

Eleanor Rand Wilner, *The Girl with Bees in Her Hair*

LANNAN LITERARY SELECTIONS 2000–2003

John Balaban, *Spring Essence:*
The Poetry of Hồ Xuân Hương

Hayden Carruth, *Doctor Jazz*

Norman Dubie, *The Mercy Seat:*
Collected & New Poems, 1967–2001

Sascha Feinstein, *Misterioso*

James Galvin, *X: Poems*

Jim Harrison, *The Shape of the Journey:*
New and Collected Poems

Maxine Kumin, *Always Beginning:*
Essays on a Life in Poetry

Antonio Machado, *Border of a Dream:*
Selected Poems, translated by
Willis Barnstone

W.S. Merwin, *The First Four Books*
of Poems

Cesare Pavese, *Disaffections:*
Complete Poems 1930–1950,
translated by Geoffrey Brock

Antonio Porchia, *Voices,* translated
by W.S. Merwin

Kenneth Rexroth, *The Complete Poems*
of Kenneth Rexroth, edited by Sam
Hamill and Bradford Morrow

Alberto Ríos, *The Smallest Muscle*
in the Human Body

Theodore Roethke, *On Poetry & Craft*

Ann Stanford, *Holding Our Own:*
The Selected Poems of Ann Stanford,
edited by Maxine Scates and
David Trinidad

Ruth Stone, *In the Next Galaxy*

Rabindranath Tagore, *The Lover of God,*
translated by Tony K. Stewart and
Chase Twichell

Reversible Monuments: Contemporary
Mexican Poetry, edited by Mónica de la
Torre and Michael Wiegers

César Vallejo, *The Black Heralds,*
translated by Rebecca Seiferle

C.D. Wright, *Steal Away: Selected and*
New Poems

For more on the Lannan Literary Selections, visit:

www.coppercanyonpress.org

The Chinese character for poetry is made up of two parts: "word" and "temple."
It also serves as pressmark for Copper Canyon Press.

Founded in 1972, Copper Canyon Press remains dedicated to publishing poetry
exclusively, from Nobel laureates to new and emerging authors.
The Press thrives with the generous patronage of readers, writers, booksellers,
librarians, teachers, students, and funders — everyone who
shares the conviction that poetry invigorates the language
and sharpens our appreciation of the world.

The Allen Foundation for The Arts

Lannan Foundation

National Endowment for the Arts

Washington State Arts Commission

THE ALLEN FOUNDATION *for* THE ARTS

For information and catalogs:

COPPER CANYON PRESS

Post Office Box 271
Port Townsend, Washington 98368
360/385-4925
www.coppercanyonpress.org

This book is set in Aldus, a typeface designed by calligrapher Hermann Zapf. The cover and title page feature the font Gilgamesh designed by Michael Gills. Book design and composition by Valerie Brewster, Scribe Typography. Printed on archival-quality Glatfelter Author's Text by McNaughton & Gunn, Inc.